TRAITS OF A CHAMPION

JOHN FREAM

Free Church Press

CLEVELAND, GEORGIA

Copyright © 2025 by John Fream

All rights reserved. No part of this book may be reproduced in any manner whatsoever without written permission except in the case of brief quotations embodied in critical articles and reviews.

ISBN: 978-1-939283-18-4

First Printing, 2025

Scripture quotations taken from the (NASB®) New American Standard Bible®, Copyright © 1960, 1971, 1977, 1995, 2020 by The Lockman Foundation. Used by permission. All rights reserved. lockman.org

Recommendations

Being a champion extends beyond mere victory; it encompasses a mindset of intense focus, hard work and maintaining a positive attitude. A true champion not only excels in their chosen field but also exemplifies qualities such as humility, integrity and a relentless pursuit of excellence. They understand that setbacks and failures are integral to the journey, using them as opportunities *to* learn and grow stronger. Champions influence others through their actions. There is no participation trophy in life. Like the song says, "There is Victory in Jesus". This book gives us a roadmap on how to be a champion in life and a champion in eternity. My friend and pastor, John Fream, is a champion in both! **Adam Bass**, Louisiana State Senator.

In *Traits of a Champion,* author John Fream does a fantastic job of putting together a challenging yet common sense blueprint for what it really means to lead well and win in life! So many rich nuggets are unearthed throughout the book, nuggets that vividly and succinctly help guide the reader to a position of confidence and trust. Fream adeptly touches on the key components necessary to be a true champion and how to honestly put them into personally practice. While highlighting real-life champions across a variety of career fields, he gently nudges the reader to consider connecting with the greatest champion to ever live, Jesus Christ Our Lord! This book is a must-read for anyone seeking to become a true champion in life. **Pastor Doyle R. Adams**, Elizabeth Baptist Church Benton, LA; Named to LA Tech Football All Century Team 2001; Named One of 50 Greatest to Play in Joe Aillet Stadium 2018; Career Interception Record for LA Tech Football.

I have known John Fream for over 30 years. He served as the unofficial chaplain of our high school football team in Broken Arrow, Oklahoma. John is a great speaker and a great person; however, the thing that impressed me most about him is that he is a super competitive person. I had the sense that every time he spoke to our team, he was attempting to give the greatest talk ever given. John has a great passion to be the best. In his book, *Traits of a Champion*, he provides a clear and precise road map to competitive greatness. This book describes the step-by-step process that anyone seeking greatness can understand and apply. *Traits of a Champion* is a book that can improve your life, your heart, and your spirit. **Rick Jones**, Assistant to the Head Coach University of Missouri; National Federation of High Schools National Coach of the Year 2012; Positive Coaching Alliance National Double Goal Coach of the Year 2016.

John Fream is one of the great champions in life and leadership today. He constantly invests in and inspires other people. This is why I want to encourage you to read his new book, *Traits of a Champion*, and share it with others. This will be a tremendous resource for teaching and equipping others to be champions. Champions build other champions, so let's do this by sharing this book with others. **Ronnie W. Floyd**, Author of *Day by Day and Night by Night* and *365 Morning & Evening Devotions for Leaders;* Pastor Emeritus of Cross Church; Past President of the Southern Baptist Convention and The National Day of Prayer.

As I read my good friend John Fream's new book, I feel like David in the valley of EIah where he knew he had to face a critical situation of very large proportions. When everyone else was afraid because Goliath was too big to hit, David saw it differently. David's faith told him Goliath was too big to miss, and he kept picking up a stone and another stone and then another. Just like the story of David, we face daunting challenges in our private, family and professional lives. This book is one of the most motivating and equipping books I've read in many years. If your desire is to be prepared for the future and to be incredible today, this is a must read. **Dr Jay Strack**, Student Leadership University, President and Founder.

The *Traits of a Champion* is one of the best models for how to embrace a complete game-plan for winning in all seasons of life. Pastor John has created a masterful playbook for what success looks like in our culture today. This is easily identifiable to Pastor John as this is not just what he teaches and preaches, but this is who he is. He knows what it takes to be a champion on the playing field, but most importantly in the "fields that are white for harvest." May God bless the impact that this book will have on everyone that strives to be a champion for the Lord every day and in every way. **Jason Rowland**, Superintendent Bossier Parish Schools.

Throughout my working career of almost 50 years, I spent nearly half of those years employed by fortune 500 companies. I look back on all the hours I spent in seminar after seminar teaching us the "secrets" of success and managing people, never once was it mentioned the power or influence of God in this respect. Pastor John does a brilliant job of aligning God's word and direction as we walk the paths of faith, family and work. Even though my work career is almost complete, this book serves as a great guide for us all, no matter what stage of life we are in to walk the path of a "Champion" as God lights that path through His word. As my pastor for the past fifteen years, Pastor John, I thank you for the influence you have had on my life and my family. **William N. (Trey) Morris III**, President Emeritus, William Morris Companies.

Being involved in Junior High and High School athletics for over 40 years, I have read several books on what it takes to be a champion. I can sincerely say the best book I have ever read on what it takes to be a champion is John Fream's book *Traits of a Champion*. John's book not only covers being a champion on the field but also in life itself. John uses personal life experiences and events to explain the traits of champion. God truly blessed me to get to Coach John in his 8th and 9th grade football seasons. John was not only a great football player but a great young man as well. After a successful athletic career, John went on to be a pastor. I am so proud of him. I often think of how many people will be going to heaven because of John Fream. In his book John talks about winning, focus, attitude, hard work, influence, not quitting, being a leader by example and most importantly being a leader and champion for eternity. I strongly recommend reading *Traits of a Champion*. I did and am a better person for it. **Steve Dunlap**, Retired Union Athletics Administrator; Oklahoma State Wrestling Champion Coach 1998, 1999, 2000, 2001, 2001; Oklahoma Chapter of the National Wrestling Hall of Fame 2005; Oklahoma Coaches Association Hall of Fame 2022.

In a world where so much is measured by success, the desire to be at the top is stronger than ever. Winning is something everyone likes to do. Are you satisfied with your current wins? In *Traits of a Champion*, Pastor John Fream combines real life experience with tried-and-true lessons from the Bible. This easy-to-read unique collection is effective for readers of any age, any industry and any stage of life. Do you want to elevate your level of success across the board? How many *Traits of a Champion* do you have? **Ivy Russell**, GSS Oilfield Supply Owner, CFO.

My good friend, Pastor John Fream, summarizes in this handy book the key principles and practices that make true champions in every field. He emphasizes that all of us have a stewardship obligation to make the most of the gifts God has given us, to walk in integrity, work hard, and strive to do our best. The mindset of a champion is clearly important. But as Pastor John makes clear, in the end, it's not just our head that makes us a success. Above all, it is our heart. **Speaker Mike Johnson,** U.S. House of Representatives.

FOREWORD
Dr. Jerry Vines

You hold in your hand John Fream's inaugural book. This one will not be the last one. Pastor Fream writes with such clarity and interest the reader will ask for more. Having the privilege of witnessing his life and ministry up close and personal, he is eminently qualified to write a book entitled *Traits of a Champion*.

Pastor Fream is a champion in life and ministry. Drawing upon his experiences as a champion athlete he gives us a volume filled with lessons and principles that are applicable to the Christian life which he establishes as traits of a champion. As he says in the opening chapter on winning "these five common traits …come from my own research, interviews, and evaluation of and with champions." The book is filled with exciting and helpful illustrations from athletics and his own personal experiences. This makes the book easy to read and helpful in one's life and ministry.

Each chapter discusses an important step in one's becoming a true champion. Each chapter explains a true definition of that step and shares some practical ways to achieve it. For instance, in the chapter on focus, Fream shares five keys to improving our focus: principles; plan; path; purpose; priorities. He elaborates these ways to achievement in a simple, understandable manner.

As I indicated earlier, Pastor Fream helpfully uses illustrations from athletics and life. In addition, he ties the traits of a champion to biblical truth, citing applicable Bible verses and examples.

Chapter eight is the crowning one in the book and the ultimate goal- Being a Champion in Eternity! Ever the faithful pastor and witnessing Christian, Fream concludes by pointing the way of salvation through a personal relationship with Jesus Christ. He shares the simple ABC steps to receiving Jesus as personal Savior. In his final paragraph he says, "Being a true champion in Christ does mean we will have the final victory…Be a champion!!!" To which I add a hearty, "Amen!!!"

Jerry Vines, Pastor Emeritus, First Baptist Church, Jacksonville, FL; President, Southern Baptist Convention 1989-1990

CONTENTS

Recommendations 3
FOREWORD Dr. Jerry Vines 9
WINNING 13
FOCUS 21
ATTITUDE 31
HARD WORK 41
INFLUENCE 47
DON'T QUIT 55
BEING A CHAMPION LEADER 63
BEING A CHAMPION IN ETERNITY 75
About the Author 81

CHAPTER 1

WINNING

As a culture, we are fascinated with champions, and we love to see them win. Champions are the Olympic athletes we see bringing home gold medals for our nation. Champions are the people we see succeeding in business. Champions are the people who soar above all others in whatever they are doing. This is not a book about the idea that everyone is a champion, and everyone gets a participation trophy. The truth is that the message of this book is the opposite. Some people excel well beyond the average person and reach the level of a champion. We see these people in the arts, in politics, in academia, and really, in all walks of life. Some people perform at a higher level than others and are successful. What sets them apart? Is it only their God-given abilities or are there other things involved that make them champions?

It is my goal in this book to challenge you to be the best you can be and to, maybe, be the best period. We will wrestle with two extreme definitions of a champion: winning at all costs and everyone is a winner if you just try. The truth is not everyone wins and the world we live in is very competitive. Life is competitive and we should all quit expecting a trophy for just trying. Being a champion means getting better and seeking to be the best at what you are passionate about. Now, that does not mean winning is the most important thing. Being a champion does not mean you win all the time. Being a champion means you are not settling for average, but you are shooting for the stars even if you come up short.

Sports are and have always been a big part of my life. I love to watch anyone compete at just about anything. It was my senior year of high school in Midwest City, Oklahoma and we were in a dogfight for a state championship. We were at half time and my coach told us we were going to win and let's just go take care of business. As we got on the field to warm up for the second half, it seemed everyone was a little tense. You see, our high school had been in the state championship many times but had come up short. In town the week before there was talk of a "monkey on our back." You do not think you hear that stuff or even believe that stuff until you are in a tough spot. The thoughts of blowing it start creeping in. Coach gathered us before we headed to our sidelines and told us to focus on winning and not worry about losing. Well, we did go on and win the 1985 Oklahoma 5A State Football Championship.

Just about everyone wants to win but not everyone does. What separates champions from non-champions? Is it luck? Is it all about talent? What exactly are the key ingredients to being a champion? What are the common traits of a champion?

Fast forward to the year 2000 and I was volunteering with Rick Jones and the Broken Arrow Tigers football team. I did not have an official role, but Coach Jones had asked me to speak to his team every Thursday night at the team dinner and talk to them about what it means to be a true champion. While I knew what it meant to be a true champion, it was my goal to find out and study the common traits champions possessed. What were the common traits of championship teams? What made some people champions in business while others were not? What made some ministers champions while others remained average or good at best?

I think we live in a culture that downplays competition. In many cases, competition is even frowned upon, and everyone gets a "participation trophy". There is some good in promoting a "participation trophy" and competition can get out of hand sometimes. The reality is that life is a competition. While we may not always compete against others, we may be competing against ourselves.

When my daughter was playing basketball, she was very competitive. She was a decent athlete of average height, but from the time she was little, she dominated because she was so tough and competitive. The summer before her senior year she was invited to a college camp as a recruit. There were 125 junior and senior girls there for a two-day very competitive camp. They put every girl in a one-on-one tournament and/then put every girl on a 6-man team to compete against the others. Finally, they had two teams of all-stars to play in a final game. Without bragging too much, my daughter made it to the finals against a 6'2" girl and lost by one point, taking 2nd in one-on-one out of 125 girls. Her team won the two-day tournament, and she was the leading scorer for her team. In the all-star game, her team won, and she dominated (I am bragging again) leading all scorers with over 20 points.

At the end of the camp, they gave out awards and my daughter did not get the Offensive MVP or the Defensive MVP. They gave her the dreaded "Hustle" award, i.e., "participation trophy". In very competitive sports the "Hustle" award or the "Sportsmanship" award are great trophies, but they are not Most Valuable Player. This camp was set up to find the best and the MVP trophies would identify the best.

When we got to the car to load her stuff, she threw away her "Hustle" trophy and slammed the door as she got in the car. Now there were some great lessons to learn for her and me as well. I just let her simmer for a while on the way home and then we talked. We talked about life not being fair and stuff like that, but mostly I just listened to a girl who wanted to win. The truth is that the girls who got the MVP awards were being recruited heavier than my daughter by this coaching staff. My daughter knew she had dominated the two "MVP's", and she was not at all satisfied with the participation trophy.

You may be thinking that maybe we took basketball a little too seriously. We honestly did not, and I did not talk to my kids about their sports unless they brought it up. But we did talk about winning and not settling for participation trophies. I am afraid many people go through life happy to just get a "participation trophy". They go through marriage and just expect a participation trophy. They are happy to get the participation trophy in their Christian Walk. The world does not need Christians to just participate. They need Christians to be champions. Your marriage and your family need you to be a champion. Paul speaks to this in 1 Corinthians 9:24, "Do you not know that those who run in a race all run, but only one receives the prize? Run in such a way that you may win."

My daughter chose not to play college basketball but did graduate from college in four years with her BS in Business Marketing and her MBA. She is a wife and mom who loves Jesus and loves serving her church. She is in sales in a very competitive area and killing it. She is a champion her mom and I are very proud of.

In this book, it is my goal to talk about the common traits of Champions. Whether in sports, business, arts, Christianity, or just life, what makes a champion? So, get ready to be challenged and get ready to throw away your "participation" trophies. The world you live and work in rewards champions and I hope that is your goal. Remember, you do not deserve anything. As a Christian, I am so glad God did not give me what I deserve. I talk with people all the time and it seems everyone thinks they deserve recognition or greatness since they tried. While that is good for kids, you need to forget that nonsense and get out there and win! Champions win!!!

So, what makes a champion? Why is Michael Jordan the greatest NBA player of all time? What made Sam Walton a champion businessman? What made Billy Graham the greatest preacher this generation has seen or probably will see? When you look at champion-performing people and championship teams, they all seem to possess some common traits. They all seem to have some things beyond their God-given abilities. They may not be the best athlete, the smartest, or even the best looking, yet they have learned some key things that make them succeed. Notice that I said, "learned." Anyone can be a champion! Anyone can learn and grow into a champion. Let me put it in a more personal way. You can choose to be a champion! So, let's look at what makes these great champions.

Just a reminder that these five common traits can be called and categorized in many ways. As I looked at many types of champions these are the five most common that I found. This list comes from my own research, interviews, and evaluation of and with champions.

Winning is not everything. Champions work and prepare to win at whatever they are doing. That is a fact. If you want to be a champion, it should be your goal to win at whatever you are doing. Here is some simple truth though, no one wins every time or all the time. Champions do not win all the time, but they try to. Losing does not defeat them; it only motivates them to be and do better. Champions in life know this life has losses, but they do not allow those losses to beat them. Champions win because, even in a loss, they find a way to win. Let that sink in, and we will talk about that some more.

On a side note, it is my goal for these common traits speak to you regardless of your beliefs. I will be referencing the Bible often and coming from a Christian perspective. If you do not believe the Bible and are not a Christian, at least look at these common traits and see if they challenge you. If you do not believe the Bible is true, you must admit that it is a great book full of great wisdom and has withstood the toughest test of all: the test of time. If you are not a Christian, please understand my story. I did not grow up in church and did not become a Christian until 1991. Most of what I learned about being a champion came before I was saved, and what I learned was affirmed by my Christian faith. So, take a minute and look at these common traits. Who knows? You may even learn to see some value in the Bible and Christianity.

Why is it important to deal with character and values? Recently I have been working with a group of young champions. These young men were all high school athletes, and most were being recruited to play college football. We met one Sunday night a month for a year, and these twenty young men were taught the traits of a champion. They also heard from champions in sports, business, education, and faith. They got to hear from one of the most successful businessmen in Louisiana. They also got to hear from the National High School Coach of the Year. They heard from an Olympic Medalist and an NFL running back. They listened to a very successful politician. They listened to a pilot talk about his missions flying for the United States Air Force with a B-52 in the background. They got to hear from pastors all over Northwest Louisiana, along with many other coaches, business leaders, educators, and college athletes.

Let me tell you why I started the "Champions Network". My son was being recruited and many of his friends were as well. These young men were being trained in their sport and even had specialized training for them. They had strength coaches, speed coaches, and agility coaches. They were trained in everything physically that you could imagine. The thing they were not getting was specialized character and spiritual training.

Go back to the 2015 NFL Combine when one of the top prospects failed a drug test. As I listened to experts talk about the problem, I heard one analyst advise future NFL draft prospects with some terrible advice. He told future draftees they did not have to worry about being good; they needed to focus on not being bad. I could not believe what I was hearing. The bar of excellence for champions was no longer to be great. It was not even to be good; it was to not be bad. I thought this was some of the worst advice I have ever heard. I went to area high schools and met with coaches to sell my vision of developing young men to be champions on and off the field. I was given twenty-two athletes, and along with several other men, we began "Champions Network". Out of the twenty-two guys we had, many did go on to play college football in all Divisions. To this day, I still talk with many of these guys, and they are champions on and off the field.

It is important for anyone who wants to be a champion to know they can do it. I will never be an NBA champion, but I can be a champion in my field. I will never be a champion business leader, but I can be a champion at home. I will never be a champion in many areas, but I can make the choice to be a champion in my life. Being a champion is a choice you must make, and then you must get after it. It will not happen by chance! It will happen if you put your head down and get to work.

"Anyone can be a champion! Anyone can learn and grow into a champion"

Chapter 2

FOCUS

I must be honest and tell you I have a very hard time staying focused. I am a leader and a visionary with trouble seeing details. I have learned to surround myself with people who are laser-focused on the details. When I was a kid, they had not yet diagnosed children with Attention Deficit or anything else like that. My dad had a swift way of reminding me to stay focused. My mother would keep in touch with my teachers, and they would let her know about my attention and behavior. I was not a bad kid; I just could not sit still. I have no idea how kids stay still in school now with no recess or very little recess. My dad would tell me that staying focused was a discipline I needed to work on, and he would help me, if you know what I mean.

No matter what method used, a child must learn to have the self-discipline of staying focused. I know many adults who cannot stay focused long enough to finish much of anything. Adults must learn to have the discipline of staying focused in many areas of their lives. Champions must learn to be focused, or they will not see the success they hopefully desire.

Focus is our first trait. Champions have the ability to be incredibly focused on what they want to accomplish. One of my favorite people to study is a guy in the Old Testament of the Bible named Joshua. Joshua was a great leader of the Jewish people shortly after their exodus from slavery in Egypt. If you have ever seen "The Ten Commandments" with Charleston Heston or read the story in the Bible, you know Moses was probably one of the greatest leaders in history. While that may seem like an overstatement, let me remind you several million people were set free from hundreds of years of bondage. They were now out on a journey to their "Promised Land", and it would not be easy. They were now a nation without a country and Moses was their leader. They cried and whined even though God showed Himself faithful to them with food, water, and protection. Moses led this nation of millions to their home while leading them to know God in a powerful way. Moses died, and Joshua became the leader as the Hebrews were just short of the Promised Land.

I do not know about you, but it is so much easier to begin a leadership role after a bad leader than a good leader. I remind preachers, coaches, and all leaders it is way better to replace a dud than to come after a stud. Joshua could have focused on following the greatest leader these people had known. He could have focused on the battles that lay ahead of them. He could have focused on organizing a nation and the temptation to please the people. Joshua did not focus on any of that, but instead focused on getting the people to the Promised Land. Joshua knew what God had called him to do. He had been trained and mentored by a great leader in Moses. Joshua was intensely focused on God's purpose for his life and God's calling to lead God's people. Joshua knew what to focus on and he was a champion leader for the people of Israel.

Marriage is hard work, and unfortunately, too many are ending in divorce. Marriage is the process of taking two completely separate lives and slamming them together. One thing that could help everyone's marriage is to take the time to focus on your spouse and focus on having a great marriage.

At our place of work, whether we are the employee or the employer, we need to focus on being our best at that job. Focusing on being great at our job will lead to more success and, I believe, make you feel more satisfied. We must focus on being our best at anything we want to win.

Long-term, consistent winning does not happen by chance or circumstance. Winning and being champions comes by focusing on whatever you want to win.

Recently, my son and I had the privilege of target shooting with a trained expert. By trained expert, I mean he is the sniper instructor for the state police where I live. He has trained for years with military and police units all over the world. You could say that he is a champion sniper. We had several bad shooting habits that he wanted us to fix. The one I struggled with the most was staying focused down range after taking the shot. He kept telling me to follow my shot through the scope of the gun. He had us taking shots at a target one thousand yards away. Now understand one thousand yards is over a half mile, and the target can hardly be seen with the naked eye. Shooting something that far takes intense focus on the target. You cannot guess or just throw a shot out there. You must focus on wind, drop, and other factors that affect your shot. It takes intense focus to hit your target at that distance. We found it took just as much focus at closer targets if you want to be a great shooter.

I enjoy shooting, and the one thing you learn very quickly is you better take good aim before you take the shot. Many people live their lives without aiming. They just live their lives with no focus and then draw a bullseye around the area they land. A shooter would never just shoot with no aim and then draw a bullseye where the bullet hits. Great champions understand they must take aim and have their focus on the target before they shoot. Champions know what they are after, and they aim to hit the bullseye of accomplishing what they are after. They have the ability to stay focused on their goal. They achieve great things and get wins because they do not get bogged down with things that cause them to lose focus.

Here are five keys to improve your focus.

1. Principles – You are made by God for God to glorify God. People have many ideas about why we are here. Most people think we are here for ourselves and to be the happiest we can be. Let me say that we should never be our own focus, and happiness should never be our target. The target is to fulfill what God has called and equipped you for. Having principles means that you are aiming your life at what God gives you to aim at. For me, as a Christian, I always set my focus on the "cross hairs" of the Gospel. Christ died for my sins and rose again so I could have a new life in Him. Let me be clear. When you aim your life with the principle of knowing God and making Him known (which is my life's aim), then it will produce happiness in your life. If you are not a believer in God, let me double dog dare you to give God a try. Honestly seek to know Him, and He will make Himself known to you. It would be a huge disservice for me not to tell you this great truth. Yes, I admit there are many great champions who do not know God through Jesus Christ, but the greatest principle in life is God loves you and has a plan for you. I believe the greatest championship to be accomplished is to know Him, to live in His purpose and plans, and to walk in the path He has for you. Knowing God and following Him does not guarantee you will not have problems, and it does not guarantee you will win at everything. Knowing God guarantees the ultimate championship of eternal life, which will bring you more than happiness; it will bring you joy.

2. Plan – Have a plan for your life. Have a plan to make your marriage better. Have a plan to be a better parent. Have a plan to be a champion in whatever you are seeking to be a champion. Have a plan to get better. When I was young, I was challenged with the idea that "leaders must be readers". It became my plan to read at least four books a month. I am a terrible reader, but I have worked very hard on this plan to get better. Getting better or being a champion will not happen without a plan to make it happen. A plan also helps you evaluate the progress of your work. I can remember setting out on road trips with my wife and having only an atlas we got from Walmart. I would sit down the night before and plan our trip, mapping out the roads and highways we would take to get to our destination. Then the internet came, and you could map your trip online and print it off with turn-by-turn directions to guide you on your trip. Now I can get in my car and just ask my phone to give me directions. It will then give me detailed directions to my destination. Planning is my map to arrive at the destination I desire. When was the last time you sat down and planned out something in your life? Let me challenge you to set some goals for your life, work, marriage, and whatever else you are passionate about. Then, write out a detailed plan of how you will complete these goals. Of course, plans can change, just like we have detours on our trips, but work the plan. If you want to be a champion in anything in your life, you better have a plan, or you are planning to fail.

3. Path – Know your life's path is not like anyone else. You may have similar things in your path to other people, but you do not walk down the same path. Your path is unique for you. You have a unique set of circumstances and life moments that are yours. You have a unique set of people around you. Your path is yours! God has designed your path uniquely for you. Walking your path is living the life God has given you. Along that path, you have choices to make in what direction you will go. Some say life comes down to the choices we make. Champions choose the correct path, at least, most of the time. Choosing the correct path means having the right focus. I love to hunt deer, and while that is not politically correct to some, it is a passion for me. If you know deer hunting, you know they are amazing animals and have very strong hearing, vision, and smell. Deer can hear for miles, and odd sounds in the woods give them pause. Deer can also see far better than you or I can see. Even if you are quiet and in camouflage, you are probably not beating the sense of smell. To put it in simple terms, hunting deer is very difficult, and a hunter must go to great lengths to hunt them. Deer do have some weaknesses, which is what a hunter counts on. First, once a year they have such a great desire to reproduce that they get a little stupid (now there is a great lesson for another time). Second, deer are basically lazy. They will most often find and take the path of least resistance. They like the easiest path. It is on this path hunters set up to ambush and surprise them. In life, the easiest path is often not the best path. Champions are not afraid to focus on the hard path. Identify the path to the goals you have set, and that path will help you stay focused. Of course, like our plans, our paths can change and should change sometimes. Just know, like your plan, a path should not be done on the fly but should be thought out in great detail. The difference between your plan and path is that you have less control over your path. Where you were born, when you were born, and so many other factors affect your path. Stay on your path and keep your focus. Your path should help you keep your focus. Remember, your path is unique to you, and it is not like anyone else's.

4. Purpose – So much is written about purpose, and rightfully so. If you are going to be a champion in life, family, marriage, business, or whatever, you better have principles, a plan, and a path. Probably the most important thing for you is to know your purpose. Your purpose is your focus. It is the "why" of what you are doing. Great champions and great leaders are successful because they know their purpose. Joshua knew his purpose in leading the Hebrew people. Moses had the purpose of leading God's people out of slavery. Joshua's purpose was to lead God's people into the Promised Land. Champions must know their purpose, which is their "why" of what they are trying to win. Sam Walton purposed to make the greatest chain of discount stores the world has ever seen. Michael Jordan purposed to be the greatest NBA player the world had ever seen. Billy Graham purposed to be used by God to preach to more people than he could ever imagine. Sit down and establish your purpose in life and in the goals you have set, before you make your plan and identify your path. I do not want to be just a great dad; I want to be a great dad so my kids will be great. Do you see the purpose? It is not to get a championship trophy as the number one dad. It is to set my kids up to be champions in their lives.

5. Priorities – All highly productive individuals struggle with prioritizing their lives and focus. So many things pull for champions' attention and time. To be a champion, your focus must reflect your priorities, and your priorities must set your focus. I love what I get to do for a living, and it is my goal to be a champion at it. However important, it is secondary to my family and being a champion husband, dad, and granddad. Even more important than being a champion family man is my walk with Jesus Christ. It is my greatest desire to be a champion in Christ. So, to be quite clear, a champion must sit down and make sure their priorities are clear. I keep it simple for myself; God is first, then my family, and then my work. I have a terrible time saying no to any opportunity to do ministry, speak, or just be around people. I have learned over the years the ability and the wisdom to say no to invitations or opportunities that are not priorities. Setting your priorities helps keep you focused on what really matters, which is what you really want to be a champion at.

Let us review how to improve our focus. Understand who you are and why you exist (Principle). Have a road map with directions to accomplish your goals (Plan). Travel the road before you (Path). Know the reason behind your goals and what you want to win (Purpose). Set the most important things and put them in order (Priorities). I would sit down and write these things out. Keep them and use them as a guide and a test for maintaining your focus.

Many people do not accomplish great things or accomplish anything because they get distracted by things that are not their focus. Champions usually do not burn energy and time on things that are not important to their target. When I was learning to drive as a fifteen-year-old, my dad often threw me the keys and said to get us home. This was always so fun, and I loved showing off my driving skills. One day, we were on the opposite side of Oklahoma City from where I lived. My dad threw me the keys and said, "Get us home". The problem was that I had to drive on the crosstown and through the busiest traffic in the city. As I drove down I-40 all was good until I got next to a big rig. When I got next to an eighteen-wheeler, I would drift towards the truck, not away from it like most normal people. My dad had the unusual ability to stay calm and remind me to move away from the truck and center up on my lane.

When we got home, he taught me a great lesson that champions must know in life. He taught me that I was drifting towards the trucks because I was focusing on the truck and not the road ahead of me. That focus caused me to swerve towards the thing I was focusing on. In life, we will drift towards the things we focus on. Champions understand they cannot set their focus on things that are not important to their goals. When we focus on things that are not our goal, we will drift toward those things, and our target can get blurred. Champions must eliminate the things that blur their focus. Things that blur our focus can cause us to miss our bullseye. Some things that blur our focus cannot be eliminated, but they must be held in proper perspective and not be allowed to steal our focus away from our targets.

Things that can blur our focus:

Too many goals – Champions have specific targets and not too many of them. Principles, plan, path, purpose, and priorities will help narrow your focus. Highly successful people do not try to be great at everything. Champions keep their goals to just what they are passionate about. Now, you can be great at many things, but many things better not take your focus.

Too much me – Believe it or not, selfishness and focusing on self will blur your goals/targets. Being focused and driven does not mean you have to be selfish. It is easy to become selfish and self-centered when you are focusing so hard on things. Let me encourage you to fight selfishness with all your might. I have two simple questions to test myself about my selfishness. Who am I trying to win for, and who do I think of first when I think about what I am focusing on?

Loose or relaxed morals – As Christians, we have the Bible and the Holy Spirit to guide us on right and wrong. Champions are people of high character and good morals. A Christian can be assured that sin will blur their goals/targets. People who are not religious can also know that low character only stands to blur your focus/targets. How many champions are sidetracked or flat-out benched because of a vice in their lives? I am not trying to preach, and I do not want to name vices for you to get rid of. For a Christian, just hold it up to God and ask Him if it should be in your life. For a person who is not a Christian, does this vice hurt or blur your focus?

Bad Theology – "Wait, what?" you might say. Not having the right view of God will certainly blur your targets. If you do not believe in God or have a wrong understanding of God, it will cause your focus to be wrong. Your view of God will affect your aim and will blur your focus. I know some of you may not like this, but I could not live with myself if I kept this truth from you. God is the Creator of this world, and He sent His Son to die for my sins. That helps keep everything in proper focus for me. I hope you will at least think about it.

I love to see people compete and do their best. It drives me crazy to see people do something halfhearted or with half effort. Ministry is my lane, and I see so many guys going through the motions. In ministry, you can be the busiest guy in town, or you can be the laziest guy in town. While I do not recommend being the busiest, it is sad to see people say they want to be champions in ministry without trying to be the best. So, let me speak to my ministry friends. There is nothing spiritual about being less than the champion God made you. There is nothing spiritual about focusing and settling for a "participation trophy". As I heard a great preacher say many years ago, "Time is short, hell is hot, and the Gospel is truth". Ministers should learn to focus and focus on being a Champion for Jesus Christ. Quit settling, and let's go!

"Long-term, consistent winning does not happen by chance or circumstance. Winning and being champions comes by focusing on whatever you want to win."

Chapter 3

ATTITUDE

As a kid, my grandfather got me interested in bird watching. We would sit out in his backyard with a book and binoculars watching all kinds of birds. As an adult, I am still fascinated by birds, especially the larger species of birds. It has been my observation that birds are a lot like people in many ways. Turkey hunting is one of my favorite things to do, and they are magnificent animals. While they are smart, they seem to be paranoid. Their head is constantly moving, and they are constantly looking around for trouble. While they can fly, they seldom do and usually spend their time walking and strutting. They are also angry birds and fight quite often. People who act like turkeys often never sail to great heights and spend most of their time on the ground, paranoid or afraid to soar. It would appear that turkeys have bad attitudes.

The next key trait of champions is their attitude. Champions understand that a positive "can do" attitude is required for success. I am not talking about an unrealistic head-in-the-sand mentality. Great champions in business, sports, and all areas know that their attitude is critical for success. People may not have a ton of talent or even be the smartest person in the room, but they can control the room with their positive attitude. Champions do see the negative, but they choose to remain positive even about the negative. Having a "can do" attitude means thinking and believing you can get something done.

Now, we all know there are some things we cannot do. No matter how positive I am, I will never be able to sing in front of people, at least so they would want to hear. I am talking about a positive attitude that says, "I am excited to try, and I probably will win." I am talking about having an attitude that says, "I am all in and super excited to be all in." You might be thinking we are talking about a cocky, arrogant attitude. No, that is not what we want. Champions are confident without being cocky. There is a fine line between believing too much in "self" and believing in yourself with humility. It is so close to the edge that most of us are a win or compliment away from cocky.

A great champion who has influenced my life is Dr. Jay Strack. Dr. Jay is one of the best communicators I have ever heard. No matter what setting he is put in, he can connect with his audience like few people I have seen. He is passionate about helping young people become champions. As the founder of Student Leadership University, he trains teenagers to become great leaders in whatever field they end up in. He has two great sayings he always uses that we all need to hear. He always tells the students in his program it is "time for the little boy or little girl to sit down and for the man and woman to stand up." My favorite thing he teaches these young people is "your attitude determines your altitude."

There are so many things in ministry, business, sports, marriage, and life that we cannot control. One of the things that everyone can control is their attitude. Champions possess a winning, positive attitude. This attitude says, "I can be a champion and enjoy the road to that end." This attitude says, "Put any obstacle in front of me and I will overcome it with a smile on my face." This attitude says, "I can and will win at whatever I am doing and have a blast doing it."

No matter how many shots Michael Jordan missed, he believed he could and would hit the winning shot. The founder of Walmart, Sam Walton, lost his first store due to a mistake in the contract. He remained positive and determined more than ever to be a champion. Billy Graham is one of the greatest preachers ever. People loved to be around him, and presidents sought his company because he was a godly positive man.

Everybody wants to be around positive people, and nobody wants to be around a negative person. I call negative people "stinkers". Their attitudes stink. When they come around, they can make everything around them stink. Attitudes, positive or negative, are very contagious. Just ask a coach of a championship team about the team's attitude. I will guarantee you the team had leaders who were positive and uplifting in their attitudes. Losing teams will almost always have a "stinker's" attitude. Unfortunately, they probably had negative attitudes to begin with, and that is why they are losers.

Attitude is often the difference between what you succeed at and what you fail at. I am not talking about mind over matter stuff. I am talking about being a champion by having a positive attitude in ups and downs.

As a leader during the COVID-19 pandemic, I found that people around me fed off my attitude. With my staff, it was important that I stayed positive through the crisis. Now, that does not mean I was not real and concerned with the danger of the virus. Even dealing with the tragedies and difficulties, I made myself choose to be positive. When we were in the stay-at-home order for seven weeks, my staff was getting discouraged. We were all anxiously waiting for our Governor's order to reopen. We left a meeting knowing the announcement would happen that evening. When we got back to the office after the stay-at-home order was extended, I knew my staff was looking for my reaction. While I must admit I was frustrated, I chose to be positive and press on with a "can do" attitude. My staff could have gone either way but fed off me and left that day with an onward and upward attitude.

People in business love to be around winners and people with positive attitudes. As an employer who hires people, I can assure you a great attitude is critical before I hire anyone. I want employees that have positive, "can and will do" attitudes. I can remember watching a news program while in college in the late 80s. It was a report about people who live to be over one hundred years old. Everybody had something different to share about the key to living that long. One guy said he had never drunk alcohol before. Another guy said a glass of scotch every day was the key. One lady never ate red meat, and another said bacon every morning was the key. The story reported that none of these people had much in common except they were all very positive people.

A good attitude can sometimes turn your problems into blessings. We cannot control all that happens around us, but we can control how we react to the things that happen around us. We can control our attitude and champions either have or learn to have a positive attitude.

Look in the mirror at your face. Most people, when they are relaxed, have a frown on their face. It takes effort and muscles to smile. Your attitude can begin to change with something as simple as a smile. I double-dog dare you to take one day and smile at everyone. I bet you a nickel that your day will be better, and you will make countless other people's days better.

My good friend Rick Jones left Broken Arrow and became the head coach at Greenwood High School in Greenwood, Arkansas. He has been named the National High School Coach of the Year twice. He has won many State Championships and is truly one of the greatest champions I have ever been around. His team had a rule that during practice no one was allowed to say the word "hot". It was obviously very hot during the early days of Fall Camp in Northwest Arkansas, but they were not allowed to say it. Rick believed that if their mouths said it, that would lead to negative attitudes. Rick even got his team to have pride in what they were doing and outworking their opponents. While other teams complained about the heat, Rick's team stayed positive about the opportunity to get better every day, no matter the weather. It was not really a "mind over matter" situation, but his players just chose to be positive. Champions smile and have positive attitudes.

So, what makes us have bad attitudes? Sometimes life is tough and even tragic, and I get it's tough to be positive in those moments. I still believe the sooner you can find your positive attitude in tough times, the better off you are going to be. Here are some of the most common things I think can give people bad attitudes.

1. Failing to admit wrong. Inability to admit wrong can make people stinkers. Champions are not afraid to admit when they are wrong and even apologize. If you are not apologizing for mistakes, then you are not trying. People who see themselves never doing wrong and always spinning things to make themselves right are usually the people with the worst attitudes.

2. Refusing to forgive. Holding a grudge is an art form for some people. I say life is too short to hold onto grudges. The Bible says that if I do not forgive, then I am the one being hurt. Unforgiveness hurts the person who holds the grudge, and it is like a cancer in them (Mathew 18:21-35). Some people are the victims of horrible things that have been done to them. Choosing to forgive the person that hurt you does two things for the one forgiving. First, it sets you free of that person hurting you anymore. Second, it is you acting like Jesus, and that is always a good thing. People who say they cannot and will not forgive will have their attitudes soured.

3. Harboring petty jealousy. People who are jealous of other people's success will almost always have terrible attitudes. If you watch champions, they do not mind other people succeeding, and even love seeing other people succeed. Champions not only like to see others win, but they also work to help others get the win. Choose to rejoice over other people succeeding and let it serve as a motivation that you can as well.

4. Catching the "me" disease. People who think that everything is or should be about them have some of the most negative attitudes. The fact of life is that very little in life has to do with them and that upsets someone that is so focused on themselves. Contrary to what most people think, true champions do not focus on themselves. The truth is that you should live your life with God first, others second, and yourself third. That will give you a positive attitude.

5. Maintaining a critical spirit. People who think they are here to critique everything and everybody are losers. I know that is terribly blunt, but that does not make it less true. Champions find the good even in the bad. Now, that does not mean champions are clueless. It just means they make a choice not to be critical of everything. Critics are for the movies and not for champions. If you look at everything as a critic, you will absolutely have a stinky attitude. Now, that does not mean champions do not evaluate and honestly assess things. Champions do not look at everything with a critical attitude. They look at things and evaluate with a positive "how can we fix this" mindset. They see the problems and shift to change and improve. Losers criticize with no plan or intent on improving. They just criticize to be critical.

6. Desiring personal glory. People are fickle, and they will applaud you one moment and boo you the next. If your motivation is to get people's approval and have personal glory it will only lead to disappointment. Your attitude will be good when they are cheering and bad when they are booing. Champions learn to stay above that stuff and see the big picture. It is OK to have people's applause, but that will not be a champion's motivation. Champions take criticism and know that there can be truth in the criticism. People who are not champions will not take criticism because it is the personal glory they are after. They are too insecure to allow criticism or allow others to receive applause. Champions do not need the applause and approval of others to maintain a positive attitude.

So, the question is, how do I fix my attitude? How do I get a champion's positive attitude of "can do"? I tell people all the time, to fix their attitude, just follow the "5P" rule.

Pray – The number one thing that happens in prayer is it aligns our hearts with God's heart. Praying and talking to God fixes our attitude and helps us see things the way God sees them.

Praise – Recognize the good even in the bad. Start by making a list of the things you are thankful for and praise God for those things. Praising God will fix your attitude quickly.

Practice – Choose to be positive and make a conscious decision to do it. It takes practice and usually starts with our words. Speak positive things to people and avoid negative talk with people.

Perform – Get some quick wins in your life. Getting wins will absolutely fix your negative attitude. Lose some quick weight. Finish a project. Spend a day just saying positive, affirming words to everyone you talk with.

Perceive – Learn to have what I call, a "ten-thousand-foot view". Seeing the big picture is critical for champions. Losers and bad attitude folk do not see the big picture. They only see the problem or task right in front of them. I tell college students to make sure they have a "ten-thousand-foot view" to see the future and what can be. Do not just focus on that hard class that will only last for a few months. Christians, of course, must learn to see as God sees. Or at least try to see as God sees. That will only happen as you spend time with God and allow Him to reveal Himself to you through the Bible and prayer.

Back to my love of birds, the most fascinating bird in the world to me is the American Bald Eagle. When you think of a positive "can do" attitude, you do not have to look further than the eagle. The eagle uses the pressure and winds of a storm to climb to new heights. They stay above the muck of what is going on below them and soar in the clouds. Yes, they come to the ground level, but it's to great heights that they return. Champions must be like eagles and soar where others will not.

One of my favorite Bible stories is about a boy named David. Before he would be king and lead his nation, he was a shepherd. He was also the youngest of his house with many older brothers. While his brothers were off to war, David stayed home to tend his father's flock. During this war, David ran an errand to his brothers on the front line of the war. Upon his arrival, he found the Israelites afraid and huddled in their camps. In the middle of the battleground was the enemy's champion. This man was a giant and stood over eight feet tall.

When David arrived and heard the foul-mouthed Philistine bad-mouthing his nation and God, it upset him. He wondered why no one went out and shut the Philistine's mouth. David was challenged to go himself, and he quickly accepted the challenge. Now David was not a warrior and did not have warrior's training. However, he did have a champion's "can do" attitude. Most of all, he had faith in his God. You probably know the story, but David went to the field and killed the giant named Goliath. Now, that is a great, positive "can do" attitude.

Champions learn to have an attitude like David when they face whatever they are in. Champions believe they can defeat the giants. Champions have a positive attitude that allows them to succeed. Where did David get his great attitude? He had to come in the faith God had built him. David was not the first choice to become king. As a matter of fact, all his brothers were considered while he was in the pasture with his father's flock. David had something his brothers did not have. He had God's hand on him and God's calling to become the King of Israel. David had great faith, and I believe that great faith gave him a positive "can do" attitude.

One of my favorite and most positive champions in my life is Coach Ronnie Coker. As I write this, Ronnie is fighting colon cancer. Coach Coker has been a State Champion baseball coach and served many years as one of the best Athletic Directors I have ever seen. Ronnie has always been able to positively challenge people, especially young people, in an incredible way. Today, he is retired and fighting cancer, but he still seeks to spread a positive message every chance he gets. His catchphrase was recently put on a t-shirt and given to every football player in our school system. His phrase that every athlete in our area knows is "Win the Day". As simple as it is, it defines Coach Coker's mission to spread the love of Jesus and to influence people to have a "can do" attitude.

My son played football at the school where Ronnie served as A.D. My son loves to tell everyone how Coach Coker would see him every morning and tell my son to get two percent better today. Occasionally, he would remind my son if he got two percent better each day, he would be one hundred percent better in fifty days. Now, that is the champion's attitude.

So, what can you do to get two percent better each day? It is Coach Coker's belief and mine that if you get better and get some wins, your attitude will become champion-like.

Try some of the ways below to get some quick wins and get two percent better each day. (Unfortunately, Coach Coker ran out of time with cancer, but he did win in eternity!).

- Lose five pounds
- Start working out
- Finish a project
- Read a book
- Send fifteen encouraging texts to fifteen people for ten days
- Pay someone a compliment
- Smile more
- Learn something new
- Take a walk and talk to God
- Get up thirty minutes early and accomplish something
- Drive more courteous

Remember having a positive, "can do" champion's attitude is a choice you make. Also remember champions have this kind of attitude.

Champions understand that a positive "can do" attitude is required for success.

Chapter 4

HARD WORK

The next common trait of champions is hard work. You will not find a successful lazy person. As a matter of fact, successful people have a great work ethic and know how to work. Hard work helps average people be above average. Hard work helps people with limited talents be champions. I often tell my kids and young people to learn how to work hard. The ability to work hard will push them way ahead of their peers. I heard a story years ago that goes something like this.

A man had three sons, and all three of his sons worked for a friend of the family. The man they worked for owned an import and export business. The dad was talking to his sons, and to his surprise, the three sons all made very different wages. One son was paid one thousand dollars a month. Another son was paid two thousand dollars a month. Finally, the third son was paid three thousand dollars a month. The dad ran into the family friend who employed his sons and asked him why the pay differences. The company owner asked the dad if he had a few hours to come down to his company, and the dad did.

Once arriving at the company, the owner called the first son and asked him to check on a shipment. In a few minutes, the son who was paid one thousand dollars called the owner and told him all the details of the shipment. The owner then called the son who was paid two thousand dollars and asked him about another arriving shipment. That son reported the shipment was in and already put away in neat order and ready to be sold. The owner then called the son who was paid three thousand dollars and inquired about yet another shipment. That son reported the shipment had arrived and had been put up. He also reported that he had already sold what had arrived and already ordered another shipment of those goods. After that phone call, the owner asked the father if he had any more questions. The father of the three sons thanked the owner and left, knowing why his sons were paid different wages.

While the story is simple and easy to understand, the fact remains that hard work pays off. Hard work and success are married, and you cannot separate the two. Most people can work hard at what they love to do. Champions work hard at what they love to do. They also have the discipline to work hard at what they do not love doing. I often tell people when they know what they love to do, are equipped to do it, and are good at it, that is their "sweet spot". Champions know their sweet spot and tend to overwork in that area. They also understand they must work hard in the areas that are not in their sweet spot. Hard work is an absolute must for champions.

For true champions, the balance is not if they work, but it can be overworking. It can be a classic case of burnout due to being a workaholic. Champions know that working hard and then shutting it down is critical. When you have a focus and are getting after it, remember your priorities and learn to work smart. Our attitude about work is huge as we see the value of working hard. Workers must set boundaries about work and know when it is time to shut down. Leaders can be the busiest guys in the organization, or they can be the laziest. Champions learn not to be either but lean to being the busiest.

Here are some words that come to mind about work.

Necessary – Hard work is not an option for those who want to be successful. I am not good at math but let me give you a simple equation. A + Hard Work = Success It does not matter what "A" is. You can fill "A" with talent, creativity, intelligence, charisma, or whatever.

A natural process of hard work is winning. Hard work pays off, usually not immediately. You can be the smartest person in the world, and if you do not work hard, people of lesser intellect will outperform you. You can be the best athlete in your sport, but people with less ability will beat you if they outwork you. It does not matter how much personality you have; you cannot get away from work. Hard work is absolutely necessary, no matter how much talent you have. Success and winning must come with hard work.

Purposeful – Champions learn to work towards their focus as opposed to just being busy. People can either work smart or work stupid. Champions learn to work hard but make sure the work has a purpose. Champions are not busy to just be busy. Champions find the "why" in their work and get after it. Champions know what goals they are working for, and they know the steps to work to achieve those goals. Purposeful work is working hard towards goals and not getting bogged down with busy work. Most champions play hard because they work so hard. Hunting is a huge passion for me and when I do get to hunt, I am all in. Working hard at play happens because hard work is a huge part of a champion's makeup.

Blessed – God blesses hard work! Building character is a natural result of hard work. I believe that God made us to work and to work hard. I believe that God warns us that laziness is a character flaw that will only lead to our distraction. So, if laziness brings defeat, it makes sense that hard work brings victory. A person who works hard feels better about themselves and feels better about accomplishing things. Without hard work, you are not as invested in something, and the victory is not as much yours. Most people call the hard work we have in something "sweat equity". Notice that it is not rest equity. Hard work makes a champion's win even more sweet. You see, God blesses hard work.

Glorious – Hard work sets a champion apart from the field and brings glory to God. Again, my life's passion and goal are to bring my God glory through everything I do. Working hard shows character and catches people's attention, the person working hard is different. Working hard can set you miles ahead of your competition and make you stand out as different. Different from the average person who just wants to do what is required or just wants to do the bare minimum. Champions are not like everyone else, and because of that, they stand out in a good way. For Christians, anytime I stand out in a good way, I want to give glory to my God. It is because of Him I accomplish anything. It is because of Him I know how to work hard. It is because of Him I have the ability to be a champion. It is because of Him I have life and breath. Why would I not want to give Him any glory thrown at myself?

Choice – Hard work is something that champions choose to do. We can choose to be lazy, average, or hardworking. It does not take great skill or talent to work hard. It takes a willingness and self-discipline to work hard. I often encourage parents to teach their young kids how to work. Do not give them everything; make them work for it. If they want something new or some money, make them work for it. Teach them the value of hard work and the rewards of hard work. Teach them they must make a choice to work hard in life, and that starts by teaching them hard work is a part of winning. Losers work at losers' pace! Average people work at average people's pace, Hard workers work at champions' pace, and they choose to do it.

In the Bible, there is a great story about the Hebrew people under the rule of the Persian Empire. Nehemiah was the cup-bearer for King Artaxerxes of the Persian Empire. He had grown in favor with the King as his personal assistant. Nehemiah examined the wall around Jerusalem and knew until it was rebuilt that his nation would not be whole. Nehemiah sought the King's permission to rebuild the wall surrounding Jerusalem. His focus was clear as he set each family to build the portion of the wall they would live behind. His plan was brilliant, as each family would make sure their portion of the wall was strong enough to protect their family. However, to execute the plan hard work was required, and Nehemiah 4:6 says, "the people had a mind to work."

When my son was young, he would spend hours outside playing and working on stuff he loved. We never had to make him go outside and play but often had to make him come in well after dark. He would be at a basketball goal and spend hours working on shots. He would come in and holler for me to turn on some lights for him. He would work hard throwing a football at targets until he could not see anymore. His work ethic even as a little kid was amazing. The main area he hated to work at was pulling weeds in a flowerbed. Now, he sweated and worked way harder and longer at football than he had to in the flowerbeds. It was a great opportunity to teach him about hard work. I told him a lot of people work hard at things they love to do. Average people work hard at the things they are passionate about. I told him that champions work at the things they love and the things they hate. While he did not love weeding flowerbeds, he still had to have the character to work hard at it.

To this day, he still can outwork most people in the weight room or on the football field as he plays in college. He does have to make himself work hard in his new "flowerbeds" which are his grades in college. Champions have a strong work ethic and know how to work hard at what they love and do not love. It was important to me to teach my son how to work hard because my father instilled a good work ethic in me. I watched my dad work hard his entire life to provide for us. He worked in Oklahoma in the oil and gas industry. If you know the oil and gas industry, you know it is feast and famine. It is ups and downs, but through it all, I saw my dad work hard.

All champions know how to work, and you cannot succeed without working hard. Michael Jordan was well known for his work ethic in practice and in getting better. The greatest basketball player in the world worked to get better. Do you think Sam Walton built his company by being lazy and not working hard? Billy Graham is the most famous preacher of our time, and his travel schedule was relentless.

He traveled the world doing crusades all over the globe. Champions work hard, and if you are going to be a champion in what you do, hard work will be in you.

As we have talked about, it really is the easiest thing for you to choose to do to be successful. Remember that champions are not born but are made, and anyone can choose to be one. So, how do you start improving your work ethic? I would suggest finding someone who works hard and watch them. Evaluate how they work and see if you can dig into the "why" of their hard work. Seek to model their work ethic with your "why". Find some accountability for your work and let someone hold you to the fire with your work ethic. Seek honest evaluation about how you are working. Ask them to hold you accountable for your work. Remember that if you choose to do something long enough, it will become a habit. So do not quit.

Put your head down and work hard to accomplish something or get a win. When you accomplish something or get that win, celebrate the win and the hard work you put into it. See the work habit you have developed and do not go back to lazy or average work ethic. Losers just do enough work to get by. Average people do the work only that is expected of them. Champions work hard!

> "Hard work helps people with limited talents be champions."

Chapter 5

INFLUENCE

Influence is one of the least talked about traits champions possess. Every great champion understands it can be just as rewarding to help others win as it is to win themselves. Winning by yourself is OK and even necessary sometimes but taking others on the journey of winning with you is even better. The truth is we are all influencers. We are always influencing others around us. The question is, are you influencing others positively or negatively? Maybe because of politics and other divisive things in our society, people can be a little resistant to influence. I have found when people trust you, and you have earned their trust, they will be open to your influence. Champions influence people around them, and they are intentional about it.

Winston Churchill's wife was said to be as witty and smart as her distinguished husband. Whether it is folklore or fact, it has been said Lady Clementine was seen by her husband talking to a street sweeper one day while the two were out. The conversation between her and the street sweeper went on for some time. Finally, Sir Winston approached her and asked her who the gentleman was. Lady Clementine informed her husband that the man was an old boyfriend. Sir Winston quipped very quickly, "So you could have been married to a street sweeper rather than the Prime Minister of England?" Clementine responded even quicker than her husband, "Why, no. If I married that man, I would still be married to the Prime Minister of England." Now that is influence.

Great champions build their lives around winning and helping others win with them. Billy Graham was the greatest preacher of this modern era and literally preached to millions around the world. Just about every United States President called him to the White House at some point in their administration. Billy Graham was named on the Gallup Poll's yearly most admired list sixty-one times, far more than any other person. The Reverend Graham was very influential with England's Royal Family. In 1995, Queen Elizabeth asked the preacher to come to the royal family's private chapel for Easter service for the royal family. Billy Graham was the champion of champions in the religious world, and he built his life on influencing other people.

I often tell leaders and champions that the greatest lesson in influence starts with thinking about who has influenced their lives. Make a list of people who have influenced your life and then write down the things they did that made them so influential. Write down the things they did that hurt their influence on you. Now, work really hard to do the things that helped them influence you and do not do the things that hurt their influence on you.

Growing up in sports meant some of the greatest influencers in my life were coaches. One of the great men God put in my life was Coach Dunlap. Coach Dunlap coached me in eighth and ninth grade. He pushed us to be our best and to work hard to win. He was a humble man who truly cared about each one of us as individuals. One Friday night, I was up to no good at a local arcade. For the younger people, that was a place you went and played video games (Google it). I made some really bad choices that night, and my bad choices were very public. When I got to school the next Monday, it was Coach Dunlap who met me, and he let me have it. His friend owned the arcade and called him about my behavior. Coach gave me some great life advice and some stern discipline. I not only received it, but I learned from it. I knew Coach loved me and cared about me. From that moment on, my behavior was very much influenced by a great man, coach, and friend, Steve Dunlap.

So, let's talk about some great qualities of people that influenced our lives.

Competence – If you are going to lead and influence people, you must know what you are talking about. The idea of "fake it until you can make it" will not work in influencing people. People need to know that you are worth following based on the fact you can get "it" done.

Humility – For us to influence someone's life, there must be a measure of humility in us. People will allow humble people to influence their lives. They may allow arrogant people to influence their lives, but it will not last. Just taking the time to influence another person's life in and of itself is a humble act.

Caring – People want to know you care before you can have your greatest influence on their lives. Caring for people is a basic concept we often forget about. The people you influence will take correction and even criticism if they know you care for them.

Trustworthiness – Trust is one of the most underrated qualities of an influencer. It allows people you are influencing to be vulnerable and open. If they trust you, and open up, they are primed and ready to be influenced. At all costs, do not break their trust.

Willingness – Influencing other people takes time and energy. It requires us to be relational and personal with individuals. Being willing is a simple choice of whether you will invest in others to see them improve.

Loyalty – As a young man, I heard a leader say the greatest thing he demands of his staff and the greatest thing he gives his staff is loyalty. I thought that was a little shallow at the time, but I have since realized he was right. It is critical we expect and give loyalty to the ones we are influencing.

Passion – People love to follow passion, and passion is so contagious. Passion is influencing and what you are influencing them towards is fuel for people to get better. People feed off an influencer's passion.

Character – Being a good person today is so underrated. Being a person of influence means you must have character. Character is defined as who we are when no one is watching. I like to say that character is just being a good, moral person.

Selflessness – People know why you are trying to influence them. They want to be influenced by someone who does not have selfish motives. Influence people for their good and not for the good they can do you.

Arguably, the greatest influencer in the Bible besides Jesus Christ is the Apostle Paul. Paul is considered the greatest missionary and church planter the world has ever seen. Paul was a strong Jewish leader who met Jesus Christ on the Road to Damascus. Paul's name was Saul, and after giving his life to Jesus Christ he was forever changed. He became an influencer for the kingdom of God. He would go on to write much of the New Testament and plant churches all over Asia and Europe. Paul's influence helped take the message of Jesus Christ to Greece and even Rome. Not only did his influence reach Rome, but his influence even reached the House of Caesar (Phil 4:22). The Bible teaches that Paul ran his leg of the race to take the message of Jesus to the world. He passed the baton on to the next generation, and they, in turn, passed it on. Today, we are carrying the same baton of the relay race. Now, that is how influence works.

To be a great influencer, we must be willing to continue personal growth ourselves. Being a great influencer requires you to continue to grow and get better.

When I first got into ministry, I had a man in my life who made me read every month. I was required to read four books a month, which was a huge stretch for me. I was not a reader, and he knew that and challenged me to "read to lead". He would remind me if I wanted to influence people's lives and take them somewhere, I needed to go there. You cannot take someone someplace you have not been. Reading is a great way to continue growing.

Great influencers read and seek to learn. By doing this, they can be a well with plenty of water. If you want to influence, and I hope you do, ask yourself, "How am I growing myself?" Take a class, read a book, or get someone to pour into your life. Make a commitment to get better yourself and never stop. Champions get better and do not settle.

One of my favorite baseball players was Tony Gwynn of the San Diego Padres. Tony did not look like a great player because he was short and a little pudgy. But if you check the books, you will see he was one of the greatest hitters the Major League has ever seen. Gwynn won eight batting titles in his career with a lifetime batting average of .338 and never averaged below .309. The amazing thing is while Tony was at the top of his game, he would be the first to arrive for Spring training. It was said while the rookies were first to arrive, Gwynn had already been at camp in the batting cage. Remember champions know how to work, and those young guys were greatly influenced by seeing Tony's hard work. They saw the best hitter working to get better.

Now, let me say a word about working with sheep and not herding goats. A good influencer means you find people who want to be influenced. It is important you find young champions who want to be influenced and who want to get better. Being teachable is such a difficult thing for young champions. I tell young people the two things you can control and will instantly set you years above your competition are hard work and being teachable. I give the people I am pouring into work to accomplish and hold them accountable. If they fail to meet the requirements, I give them the "3 strike" rule. Grace is offered for the first and second failures to meet the expectations. After the third failure, I inform them we are ending our coaching relationship. No harm and no foul. I love them and still will pray for them and seek to encourage them. However, I do move on and do not allow them to waste my time. It sounds harsh, but they will show you if they are serious about your influence.

We have been talking about intentional influence, now, let us talk about unintentional influence.

The hard truth is that we are influencing lives all the time. If you hold a position of leadership or a position people look up to, you are influencing others. People look to leaders and imitate what they do well. They also look at what leaders do not do well and, unfortunately, tend to imitate that as well. Watching influences people, and they tend to imitate what they see from others, especially those in high-profile positions. So, the lesson for all of us is that people are watching, and they will especially watch champions.

If you are a champion and think you are not influencing lives, then I think you are missing something very important. How you treat people and how you talk with people is noticed. How you work and even what time you get to work is noticed. They pick up on your attitude and catch whatever attitude you exude. People see your focus or lack thereof, and it will affect their focus. The bottom line is do not underestimate the power of your unintentional influence. I promise you people are watching you.

When my kids were young, we would go out to dinner as a family and would play a little game. The game was to see how many people in the restaurant we knew. The problem is more people knew us than we would know. You see, as pastor of a church in a community, people know you, especially in the south. Not only do they know who you are, but they watch you. My kids learned this at an early age when we were out in public, and people would come to our table to say hi. We love that as a family.

My kids also learned that people we did not know were watching. I bought my daughter a red Camaro for her sixteenth birthday. The good news was I did not have to worry about her driving, because I got constant reports from church members and people I did not know about that "little red Camaro". It worked so well that my son got that same car to get him through high school. People are watching you and ready to report on your "doings". It is a daunting thing to know that people are watching, but it is also the power of unintentional influence. Who is watching you, and how are you doing?

"Being a great influencer requires you to continue to grow and get better."

Chapter 6

DON'T QUIT

Every champion knows that losing and getting knocked down is part of competing. It is not about if you lose but when you lose. If a person never loses, then I would say they are not trying to win. If you never lose, you are stuck in a bad place of comfort and are not even competing. If you are competing and not losing, you are only competing in very low-level things. To be great and be a champion you must take on big things. Taking on big things means you will certainly face some losses. Champions take on big things and learn from their losses.

The Apostle Peter was the outspoken leader of the disciples. Jesus poured His life into many, and His ministry touched the lives of too many to count. He spent most of His time with the twelve disciples and even had a close inner circle. That inner circle was made up of three men, Peter and two brothers named James and John.

Early on, Peter took on the role of leader. He was strong in personality and was often out of line in His thoughts and questions. He also was a man Jesus praised for being a man of God with the right answers (Matthew 16:13-20). You could say Peter was well on his way to being a champion. The night the Lord Jesus was arrested, Peter informed Jesus that he would never betray the Lord. Jesus would inform Peter that he would deny Him three times before the rooster crowed (Matthew 26:34).

After Jesus is arrested and taken into custody, He is led off to the High Priest's home. While Jesus was inside the home being abused, Peter was in the courtyard of that home denying that he even knew Jesus. You even have this awkward moment when Jesus looks out a window and sees Peter in the courtyard denying Him (Luke 22:61). You talk about an epic failure and loss. Peter, who was on the road to being a champion, took one of the biggest losses a follower of Christ could have. The good news is that the Lord restored Peter, and Peter did not quit. As a matter of fact, Peter would get the privilege of preaching the first sermon after Pentecost, and three thousand souls were saved that day.

You have heard the saying that "cheaters never win, and winners never cheat". Well, I am not sure how true that is. Here is a great truth that you can take to the bank. Champions don't quit, and quitters are not champions. Quitting is not an option for those who seek to be champions.

I once was doing ministry in a downtown area of a large city when I had a wonderful talk with a homeless man. Instantly, I could tell this man was very educated and was surprised by his knowledge. After much discussion, he told me that he had graduated from law school and been married. I asked him what got him to the streets and homeless. Without missing a beat, he told me he was tired of losing. He had suffered several losses in his career and in his marriage. Losses can get us down and make us want to quit, but we must press on. Losses are just some of the reasons people quit.

As every dad should, I wanted to build into my son that he was not to be a quitter. He loved football, and no matter what happened on or off the field, he was in one hundred percent. Not only was he all in, but he would not quit no matter what. Baseball, however, was a different story. He played it to hang out with his friends and liked it somewhat. When it got hot in the dog days of summer, it was certainly on his mind that maybe he did not want to go out there. You see, most people will not quit what they love to do. Even when they experience losses, they can press on through the tough times. Quitting something you do not love is way easier to do. Champions do not quit; it makes no matter if they love or hate it. Champions know they must do the things they hate to, and that can be even more important than doing what they love.

Champions learn from their losses! One of the sweetest times of my life was playing high school football. I wish I had been a Christian during those years, but nonetheless, playing high school football was awesome. The competition and hard work, along with the camaraderie, are something I miss to this day. There is not much better than Friday night in a community that loves their high school football. I love the old saying, "I love Friday nights when you are looking for a win and Saturday morning when you have found one."

Every Saturday morning after a Friday night game, we gathered as a team and watched the previous night's game. It was a tale of two worlds. It was so fun and exciting, but it could be awful at the same moment. One play you dominated, and the next was not so good. The film never lied, and we watched every play over and over. The rough Saturday mornings were after a loss the night before. While it was tough, it was important that we watch the film and get better. Even when we won, we watched the film and learned from our mistakes. A champion watches the film and learns from the losses. As difficult as it may be, it is very important that you learn from those losses.

Equally important to learning from the losses is to move on. Champions not only learn from their mistakes, but they move on. When a champion gets knocked down, they get up. If we dwell too long in a loss, we can become losers, and nobody wants that. Winning and losing in life, business, or whatever can become a learned habit. The same is true of losing. If we are not careful and stay in our loss too long, losing can become a habit. Losing is a bad habit, and champions run from this habit. When you lose, get up and shake the dust off. You must know that there will be another day and another opportunity. Learn from the loss and get ready to win the next time.

There is such a fine line between being confident and being cocky. My two kids had great success in sports and really most of what they attempted. We built in them at a young age that their winning was in their hands. We taught them to believe they could win every time and all the time. Champions believe they can and will win. Confidence is important and believing you can win must be what champions think.

When my son was young, he had a lot of success. In his first game ever in "Pee-Wee" football, on the first play, he took the ball eighty yards for a touchdown. He experienced great wins and some losses. Dealing with the losses was something he would bounce back quickly from. The problem came with all the wins. When he won a bunch, he would have to learn as a little guy the importance of humility. You see, I wanted him to want to win. I wanted him to expect to win and believe he could win. The balance for him was not being a cocky little guy. While champions believe they can win, they are careful to remain humble and grateful. Champions must develop an attitude that they can and will win in life. They must balance that with humility and being thankful for every win that comes their way.

One of the great truths for all of us is a loss is only temporary. It does not define you and does not make you a loser. We all have difficulties in our marriages, and Lord knows I have had some losses in my relationship with my wife. I have had losses in ministry, and I have had losses in everything I have tried. The good news is they have always been temporary. A loss will only not be temporary if I allow it. Champions review the game film after a loss, get better, and keep moving forward. Champions don't quit.

So, let's talk about some great champions and their losses. Few would argue that Abraham Lincoln was not one of our nation's greatest presidents. He was a strong leader, a man of great character, and a champion. President Lincoln had some great losses in his life that made him better.

Take a look:

1832 – Defeated in Legislature race

1833 – Failed in business

1835 – Mourned the death of his sweetheart

1836 – Suffered a nervous breakdown

1838 – Defeated in race for Speaker

1840 – Defeated in race for Elector

1843 – Defeated in Congressional race

1848 – Defeated in Congressional race

1855 – Defeated in race for Senate

1856 – Defeated as Vice-President

1858 – Defeated in race for Senate

1860 – Elected President of the United States

Abraham Lincoln learned that losses are temporary, and I am sure he learned from every one of his losses. The critical thing is that this champion did not quit!

One of the greatest champions in business was Walmart founder Sam Walton. What he has done with discount stores has changed all our lives. Mr. Walton got his start in retail stores in 1945 with a Ben Franklin Store in Newport, Arkansas. His goal was to make it the best in the state, and he did just that in a few years. Due to an oversight in the contract, Sam lost his first store to the man who owned the building. Sam and his wife drove back to Northwest Arkansas with a huge loss, but he was determined to get up and not quit. The rest is history. His stores are all over the world, and he is the champion of discount retail.

I love the discussion of the greatest who ever played a sport. It is so tough to have this discussion because it is tough to compare eras. Sports in the 1960s were different from the 1970s, and the 1980s were different from both, and so on. Who is the Greatest of All Time (GOAT) in football, baseball, or whatever sport? I believe the easiest GOAT to name is Michael Jordan in the NBA. He has the championships, the points, and, most importantly, his foes on the court will even say he is the greatest. Regardless of if you disagree with me (and you are wrong), you know him to be a champion. Jordan has had many losses and missed plenty of important shots. He was even cut from his tenth-grade basketball team in high school. I am sure glad Michael Jordan did not quit.

The GOAT in my world must be the Reverend Billy Graham. Billy was the greatest preacher and evangelist of our time. Presidents sought him for advice, the Queen of England had him preach the Royal Family's personal Easter service, and he was named to the most respected list almost every year. Billy Graham preached to millions upon millions during his ministry. When Billy was first called to preach, he traveled with a traveling preacher who told him to be ready to preach at a moment's notice. Billy prepared and memorized four sermons to be ready when he was called on to preach. So, the first time to preach finally came for Billy Graham, and the four sermons he had prepared were over forty minutes each. Billy was preaching one of his sermons, but due to anxiety and nerves, he preached all four sermons and only eight minutes passed. He later admitted, "Nobody ever failed more ignominiously" (shamefully). Billy Graham failed big time in his first sermon, and I am sure many more, but he did not quit!

Speaking of champions, one of my favorites must be Winston Churchill. Mr. Churchill was the Prime Minister of England during World War II. I tell young preachers, speakers, and leaders to read everything they can about and written by Winston Churchill. He must be considered one of the greatest leaders the world has ever seen and certainly qualifies as a champion.

When Winston was a young schoolboy, he was expelled from grade school and told he would never amount to anything. The school asked him to come back and speak after leading England through the awful war. The entire town showed up at the school to hear its most famous citizen speak. The community was abuzz when Mr. Churchill approached the podium. He resolutely faced an expectant crowd and voiced with great power these few words. "Never give in, never give in, never, never – in nothing great or small, large or petty – never give in except to convictions of honor and good sense. Never give in". Then, to the amazement of all, he turned and sat down.

If you try anything, and most certainly anything worth trying, you will have wins and losses. Champions try difficult things and go for the win, knowing that a loss is possible. That loss does not stop champions but serves to make them better. Losses will either make you better or bitter. Champions choose to get better from losses. Whatever you are facing in your life, ministry, family, business, or whatever, don't quit! A quick word to Christians. The Christian Walk is not always easy and can be tough sometimes. We can even experience losses in our walk. Please pray and ask for strength, and don't quit!

"If a person never loses, then I would say they are not trying to win."

Chapter 7

BEING A CHAMPION LEADER

There is so much written about leadership, and rightfully so. Nothing is more important to an organization, team, family, or business than leadership. In my world of the church, I have seen all kinds of leaders. I have seen some of the greatest leaders the world has ever known. I have no doubt if these men were in secular business or coaching, they would be huge successes.

Unfortunately, I have also seen some bad leaders who struggle with some of the most basic truths of leadership. It is a tragedy in the church when bad leaders spiritualize their bad leadership. They do this by excusing their bad leadership with the idea that they are doing God's will. In business and sports, bad leaders are exposed very quickly, and the secular world is not near as patient as the church is with bad leaders. So, what makes champion leadership in business, sports, church, or even the home?

Let me start by talking about one of the greatest leaders the world has ever known. I mentioned him in chapter two as a great leader, and his name is Moses. The Bible tells us that Moses was born to Jewish parents who lived in slavery in Egypt. The leader of Egypt was growing concerned about the number of Hebrews in his country. Even though they were slaves, they flourished, and their numbers scared the Egyptian Pharaoh. So, Pharaoh decided that all newborn male Hebrew children would be put to death. It was a form of population control, if you will. Well, back to Moses' parents; they did not want their newborn son to die, so they made a plan. Moses' parents put him in a basket and placed him in the Nile River near where Pharaoh's daughter went to bathe, hoping she would take baby Moses as her own. The plan works so well that not only does Pharaoh's daughter take Moses as her own, but by God's providence, she gets Moses' mother to come and nurse the baby. The Bible tells us that Moses is raised in the palace of Egypt as royalty. Moses would turn his back on the Egyptians because God had a plan for him.

Champion leaders know how to focus and what to focus on. Not only do they know the focus, but they are also able to get their team to have that same focus. I am not a musician, and I wish I had learned to play some type of instrument. While I do not know music, the band or orchestra must all have the same focus. The leader must make sure they all stay focused on the same thing to make good music. It is so funny to me when an orchestra is getting set up, everyone is tuning their instruments or just playing something random. It sounds like a mess and really is kind of funny. Suddenly, the conductor will step to the podium and lead every section with the same music. He will adjust their timing if it needs to be. He will call for volume from a certain section if it is needed. When the leader gets everyone to focus on the same music, it is a joy to hear what they are playing. How do they go from all the random noise to the sweet music of a performance? It comes down to the leader. Wherever your leadership is, you must get your team to focus on the same things and make "sweet music."

Champion leaders also know how to inspire and motivate their teams. I believe great leaders set the "attitude atmosphere". Every team has an atmosphere, and winning teams have winning attitudes. I know that sounds like a "duh" statement, but bear with me for a second. Winning teams expect to win, and they have an attitude that says, "We will win and pay the price to win." Losing teams do not have winning attitudes and will often expect to lose. Leaders must set an attitude of winning in their organization. They must set an attitude of joy and an atmosphere that is positive.

Maybe you have heard it said like this: leaders must be "thermostats" and not just "thermometers". A thermometer measures the temperature, and a thermostat sets the temperature. In my house, I am the keeper of the thermostat. It is my job to make sure the temperature in the house is comfortable in the summer and in the winter. A thermometer tells me the temperature, but the thermostat is what I adjust to control the temperature in my house. Leaders must read the temperature of their organization for sure. Reading the temperature is critical in knowing your team. Reading the temperature of the team is equal to reading the attitude of the team. The reason I read the temperature is to know where I need to take the temperature. Your team has an attitude that must be read, and then a good leader sets the thermostat to adjust it as needed. Winning is contagious; a good leader sets the pace for this attitude.

I am not the kind of leader my staff does not see or must have an appointment to see me. I walk the halls quite often, and I am doing several things. First, I just like people, and I like my team. They know this because they see me, and I take time with them. Second, I am reading the temperature of my team. I want to know where their attitudes are. Third, I am acting as a thermostat and setting the temperature of my team. I walk around smiling and laughing and letting them know they can win. I am meeting with them and making sure they believe they can win. Leaders need to walk the halls of the office and be around the people they lead.

Effort and attitude are the two things that people with average talent can do to level the playing field. Effort is truly about hard work. If someone is willing to outwork everyone, then the sky is the limit for them. Average-working people accomplish average success. Hard-working people will accomplish great things and have more wins. I believe that with every fiber of my being.

In my organization, I am in a place where I do not have to do much manual labor. Not only do I not have to do it, but it is also expected of me sometimes not to do it. Now, hard work is more than manual labor but go with me for a second. When we have a huge event where several thousand people show up, I have crews of paid workers and volunteers who do most of the setup and tearing down. I am not expected to be there and to help, but you will often find me right in the mix getting sweaty and working hard. Part of the reason is I like to work; it is just part of who I am. Most of all, I do it to set an example for my team to follow. I do not expect my team to work hard and not model it myself. Hard work for your team should be expected and modeled by their leader. Hard work does not mean working "dumb". More is not better all the time; smart is better. Show your people you are willing to work hard and long but also show them the importance of working smart.

My first job in ministry was as a Student Pastor, and we were required to be in the office by eight o'clock in the morning. I was there every day by seven or seven-thirty because I wanted a head start on the day. To this day, I am often the first in the office, and I model hard work to my staff. Leaders must work hard and show their people what they expect.

Of course, the greatest thing about leadership is influence. Because of a title or position held by a leader, they can get people to do things. I call this getting people to do what they are paid to do. Remember though, we are not just trying to win but to be champions. I want my people to do more than what they are paid to do. I want them to love what they do and have a passion for it. My goal is to influence them to have a "can do" attitude and to have so much passion for what they do that I have to make them take time off.

I believe that anyone can be a champion, and it is my goal to influence them to be those champions. Influence is about pouring into people's lives. Influence is about having relationships with the people you are trying to influence. Influence is about helping people win for themselves and not just winning for you. Just a quick thought about your leadership and your influence. Look at your team and evaluate how you are doing influencing them. How well you are influencing them is easily done by their job performance. If they are on my team, I look to myself first to see how I am influencing them before I start evaluating them.

Giving away ownership to people in your organization is critical for them to have a passion for what they do. If they own it, they will do whatever it takes to win in the area they own. Giving away ownership means you must let people fail and fall. I do not let them have fatal falls if I can help it, but I will let them take a loss. That loss will build in them some very key traits of a champion. The greatest thing it will build in them, with the help of a good leader, is not to quit. Enduring through difficult times and even losses will be critical for them to be champions. You leading them through those losses will make you a champion leader.

Good leaders come alongside their team and help them win. Great leaders come alongside their team when they lose and turn it into wins. Teaching and training your people that losses are not good is important. Teaching and training them how to react to losses is even more important. It must be the culture of your organization that no matter what, this team does not quit. We have the "don't quit" attitude. That must come from their leader, who loves and trusts them. People who are not afraid to lose, although they hate losing, will go for big things. People who are afraid to lose will only do what is expected of them. If you build "don't quit" into your atmosphere, it will make your people champions, and your organization will win championships.

Why do we look at John Wooden, Nick Saban, and Bill Belichick as champions? Why do we look at Michael Jordan, Jack Nicholas, and Tom Brady as champions? Why do we look at Sam Walton, Bill Gates, and Elon Musk as champions? We look at them this way for the same reason we look at Billy Graham, Billy Sunday, and Charles

Spurgeon as champions. They all not only won big in their areas, but they led others to be champions. To be considered the best, you must be willing to help others be the best. Champion leadership is about making champions.

So, how do you become a champion leader, and what can you do to work on your leadership? I know, I know. Too many questions, but they are asked for a reason. Leaders do not always have the answer, but they know the questions that need to be asked to get the answer. God does this in the Bible.

In the beginning, when God made Adam and Eve, they sinned and blew it. Adam and Eve covered their nakedness and hid from God. I love that they hid from God as though He could not find them or because they were that good at hiding. You read in Genesis chapter three that God walks into the garden after they had sinned and calls out with a very important question for Adam and Eve. *"Where are you?"* Now, you must ask yourself, did God know where they were? Of course, He knew where Adam and Eve were hiding, He is God and knows everything. So why the question? God wanted to teach Adam and Eve to be champions and help them learn by asking them a question. Jesus did the same thing to Peter and the disciples when He asked who the people believed Jesus to be (Matthew 16). Jesus knew who and what people were saying about Him. He wanted His disciples to answer the question and learn.

You see, great leaders do not always give answers. They know some of the greatest learning is not giving answers but asking questions and letting people work out the answers. Learning is the most important thing for your team, and as the leader, you must lead them to learn. Give them questions to answer, and do not just download information all the time. When they work out the answer, it will be something they learn and know in a very deep way.

Let me give you the easiest and quickest leadership lesson in the world.

Let me start by saying it is way better to learn from other people's mistakes than your own. Write down the great qualities of leaders in your life that made them great leaders. The things that made you want to follow them. The things that made you love that person and be willing to charge any hill for that person. Your list probably includes humility, character, wisdom, love, trust, or whatever things you come up with. Now write down the bad qualities of the leaders in your life that made you not want to follow them. They probably include arrogant, cold, distant, not caring, using people, or whatever things you can think of. So here is the lesson. Do the things as a leader that you loved in great leaders! Do not do the things as a leader that you did not like in the leaders in your life.

So back to the becoming a champion leader question. You sit down and write out the top things you need to do to be a champion leader. You work out the answer and decide what you need to work on and do to be a great leader. Remember this is a book on being a champion, and I am sure there are much greater books on leadership than this. So here are some quick hitters on being a champion leader.

Evaluate more – Inspect what you expect! Do not assume that everyone on your team has the same passion and work ethic as you. Accountability to the high standard you model and expect is part of making people great. Put performance markers in your team's work and let them be involved with the markers. These markers need to be crystal clear about their job expectations. Tell them what they need to do to be a champion in their position. Then, great leaders work to help their team accomplish those markers.

Love more – Love never fails (1 Corinthians 13:8)! People need to be loved, and leaders need to love their people. In a world that is so divisive and ugly towards one another, leaders set a tone of love. Love is caring for your people and truly wanting the best for them as a person. Love is also tough and honest. Some people define love as caring for someone so much that you do not confront failures and weaknesses. When, in all actuality, love demands you confront these things. I believe that love is one of the most underrated characteristics of a leader. Your people will respond positively to genuine, pure, and consistent love. I know you must be careful in our world today, so certainly be smart and appropriate.

Listen more – Listening is an art! I do not know about you, but listening is something I had to learn and something I still must work on. Leaders need to listen to their people and what they are saying. People feel valued when they are heard. People will have more passion when they are listened to. Make sure and set up healthy avenues for your potential champions to communicate with you.

Humble myself – People do not want to follow cockiness! Confidence wrapped in humility is one of the strongest traits a leader can exude. No one wants to follow arrogance, so do not be arrogant. Be thankful and know that God has blessed you, and He alone should get the glory. Knowing who I am before my Lord makes me confident and humble.

Check my motive for helping people win – Your people will know why you want them to win! If your motive for helping people succeed is so that they can help you, check your motive. If your motive for helping people succeed is so they can make you look better, check your motive. Help your people win with the pure motive of just wanting them to win. Yes, it will help you and your organization but let them win to build their champion's traits.

Be nice to everyone, especially stinkers – Being nice to people is very underrated! Anyone can be nice to nice people. Champion leaders are nice to even the stinkers in their life. Stinkers are those people who have "stinky" negative, complaining attitudes. Correction must come, but it can be done nicely. Being nice is another underrated champion leadership trait.

Learn more – You must read to lead! Leaders must be growing themselves to grow your people. A leader will have a difficult time taking people someplace they have not been or someplace they refuse to go themselves. Get better and then demand your people to get better. Learn and then demand your people to learn with you.

Work hard – Set the pace! A champion leader knows how to work smart and hard. Leaders are the pacesetters for an organization for work. In a long-distance race, the race officials will set a "pacer" out in front of the race to keep the pace up. After a while, the "pacer" steps out, and the racers keep pace. Leaders must set the pace for their people to work hard and smart.

Be confident – People want to follow confidence! People will follow winners, but they will not follow losers long term. Leaders need to be the ones in the room with the "can do" attitudes we talked about earlier. Confidence is contagious, and leaders should be confident in what they do. Confidence is also security for your team. It makes them believe in your leadership and trust your leadership. Remember though, that confidence without wins is false confidence, and champions will not follow that long term.

Lead, but do not drive – Be a shepherd, not a cowboy! You have probably heard the comparison between eastern and western shepherds. Eastern shepherds lead their flock and care for them. They make sure the sheep are fed, protected, and well. Western shepherds drive their herds from one place to the other. Get out front and lead your people with care and strength.

Lead by example – Do what you expect others to do! I always try to show my team I am not above any work in our organization. They will see me doing just about anything that needs to be done or that I can do. They see me loving people and caring for people. They see me learning and growing. They see me doing what I expect of them. Champion leaders take the example part of leadership very seriously.

Lead by service – Do what others are not willing to do! The greatest leader the world has ever seen served people. The King of kings literally got down on the ground and washed His people's feet. I double dog dare you to read John 13:5-17.

Let's compare champions to non-champions (see the comparison chart below). This can be non-champion leaders or followers. Really, leaders need to know that not everyone they lead will be champions or want to be champions.

Champions	Non-Champions
Talk	Whisper/Gossip
Encourage	Discourage
Challenge	Complain
Make Decisions	Avoid Decisions
Work for Team	Work for Self
Evaluate	Critique
Make Changes	Gripe about Change
Love People	Attack People (especially leaders)
Give	Take
Lonely	Run in Packs
Tough on Self	Tough on Others
Self-Evaluate	Blame Others
Confronts Conflict	Avoids Conflict
Vision	Near Sighted

I think one of the top leaders I have read about has to be John Wooden. Coach Wooden won ten national titles as the coach of the UCLA Bruins Men's Basketball team. It is said that when his team first arrived every year, he would start off by showing them how to put their socks and basketball shoes on. It was new for the new guys and a refresher for the veterans. Coach felt if his team took care of the little things then the bigger things would be taken care of as well. A leader must help their organization to start well so they will finish well. Coach felt great leaders do not insist on their way but seek the best way.

Another great leader was Coach Herb Brooks. Coach Brooks led a bunch of college hockey kids to defeat the all-powerful Russian hockey team made up of professionals. You may remember it as the "Miracle on Ice" in the 1980 Winter Olympics. The Russians were unbeatable in most peoples' minds, but not Coach Brooks and his team's minds. Coach Brooks would say that great coaching and great leadership is "not putting greatness in your team but pulling it out of them".

Another great leader I did not have to read about but knew personally was a man named Jim Dawson. Jim was a friend who retired from Brunswick Outdoors to come on staff at a church where I served. He came on to help the pastor and help the church that he loved. Jim had turned Zebco Fishing Poles from a struggling company facing bankruptcy into a very successful business. Mongoose Bikes was also a part of Brunswick, and he helped turn them around. Now, he was leading a bunch of preachers on a church staff. Jim was a larger-than-life figure physically and in his personality. Jim was tough and demanded greatness as he said we are doing God's business. He also loved us and gave us the freedom to be champions in our own right.

As a young minister on staff under Jim, I learned a ton about motivating people and pushing people. He allowed you to argue with him, but his personality guaranteed you did not go too far. He allowed you to disagree, but your respect for him made you get on board. Jim could get on you pretty good, and it was OK because you knew he loved you. He gave me an open invitation to fish his private personal lake that very few people had. When I was promoted to a new position at the church, Jim was tough to negotiate with. He told me there was just not any budget money for much of a raise, even though my workload and responsibility were increasing. I told him I got it, and we would move on. Later that week, he walked in and handed me an envelope. In the envelope was a receipt for some mutual funds he had personally invested in my name. You see, Jim was a champion leader. Jim was tough, but he was fair and caring. I would have run through fire for that man, and I hope I am the kind of leader now that my people would do the same.

If you are in leadership in your organization or in your home, you can be a champion leader. Being a champion leader is learned, and it is a choice. Go for it and be the champion leader God wants you to be.

> "Champion leaders know how to focus and what to focus on."

Chapter 8

BEING A CHAMPION IN ETERNITY

Being a true champion is something that I am deeply passionate about. As a matter of fact, I have surrendered my entire life to the purpose of making true champions. True champions may sound a little arrogant but hang with me for a bit. You see, being a true champion is not about you. Being a true champion is about you giving your life to Jesus Christ.

Wait!

Stay with me and hear me out on this one because this is the one thing that matters most. I understand if you are skeptical and concerned about religion and a religious message. I am not talking about a religion, and this is not religious talk. I am talking about a relationship with the God who made everything, including you.

The Bible teaches God spoke the world and the universe into existence. You may struggle to believe that but hear me out for a second.

One of my favorite trips of all time is to Rome. That place is amazing, and there is more to see and eat than you can imagine. One of the best parts about Rome is to go to Vatican City and see all it has. My favorite part is to see the Sistine Chapel and the ceiling that Michelangelo painted. To say that it is breathtaking is a huge understatement. If you went to Rome and just saw that, the trip would still be worth it.

To think that he laid on his back for all those years painting that gorgeous masterpiece blows my mind.

I have never met Michelangelo, but I know he existed because that work of art is there to prove that he existed. If you have a painting, then you know there is a painter. History records that he is the painter who painted that wonderful work of art. I believe that he did because I see the work of art.

The same is true of the creation we see around us. If there is a creation, then there must be a Creator. Let me give you another thought. If I saw a turtle on a fence post, I would know someone was there before me and put the turtle on the post. I am assuming with good reason that a wind did not blow him up there. I am assuming he did not crawl up there. It is obvious that someone was there and placed the turtle on the fence post. I look around this world and know it did not just happen. Someone was here and made this happen.

I believe God is the Creator, and He created this world. I believe this because not only does the Bible tell me so, but because I also see His creation. I admit it does take a measure of faith on my part, and that is the point. I have put my faith in the fact that God does exist, He created everything around me, and He wants a relationship with me.

Here is the problem for all of us. God created man with free will because He loves us and wants us to have the choice to have a relationship with Him. God did not make man without the ability to choose what we would do and not do. If man had no choice, then we would be robots programmed to just do whatever He wanted us to do. That is not love. Love says you have the freedom to have a relationship with God or not to have a relationship.

In God's creation, man made a choice to rebel and go against God. That rebellion is called sin, and the Bible teaches that everyone has sinned and will sin. This world is fallen and not the original form God created it to be because of sin. God knew the first man and woman would sin and had a plan in place for us to have a relationship with Him despite our rebellion against Him.

I like to tell people having a relationship with God is as easy as **"ABC"**. Now, this is not an original thought to me and has been used by people for many years to explain how we can have a relationship with the Creator of the Universe.

"A" – *Admit you are a sinner.* Being a sinner does not mean you are the worst person ever. It just means that you have fallen short of God's laws for you. When I was twenty-three years old, I admitted I was a sinner and in need of forgiveness for my sin. I knew prior to this I had lied; I had stolen, I had done all kinds of things that were wrong. But I had never truly admitted these things caused a problem between me and God.

When God created the first man and woman, He gave them the freedom to choose Him or not to choose Him. They chose to sin, and the world fell from its original creation.

Today, we have the same freedom, and we have all sinned. That means you! Do not put up your defenses; I am a pastor of a church, and I am a sinner. Understanding that we are sinners is the first step to being really free and being a true champion. You must admit your sin has set you apart from the Creator of the Universe. God gave you free will, and you have sinned on your own. You owe a debt or penalty for the sin you have committed. Your sin has separated you from a Holy God that loves you very much.

Do not lose heart; while there is nothing you can do about this debt; God did something for you. Romans 3:23 says, "for all have sinned and come short of the glory of God." Romans 6:23 adds, "For the wages of sin is death, but the free gift of God is eternal life in Christ Jesus."

"B" – *Believe Jesus lived and died for you.* The bad news is we are all sinners and need to be saved, is blown away with the fact that Jesus came to this earth and died for every sinner. We owed a debt we could not pay, but Jesus paid our debt for us with His death.

There is an old story about a widowed man who had lost his wife to cancer. He found himself mad at God, and never being a man of faith, his anger only pushed him further away.

A local pastor would often visit him and tell him the good news of Jesus dying on the cross for this man. The widowed man finally told the pastor to quit coming by and he was never going to believe God would come to this earth and die. As much as the pastor tried to explain God's love for us, that was the reason for sending His Son, the man just could not fathom why God would come to this earth and die. The widower was an avid bird watcher and loved to watch the birds at his numerous feeders. One could even say he deeply loved the birds.

One night during a storm, he heard a knocking on his window. When he opened the blinds, he saw a little bird running into the glass, trying to get inside to escape the storm. The man went outside and tried to scare the bird into his barn, but that did not work. He tried throwing seed on the ground and having the bird follow it into the barn. He tried everything, and little bird just kept flying around in complete fear. Suddenly, it hit the man that if only he were a bird, he could lead that bird into that barn.

With that thought, the revelation of why God would come to this earth and die made sense to him. Once you understand you are a sinner, you must believe that Jesus Christ died on the cross for you. Jesus, who was sinless, died for us in our place for our sins. You owed a debt to God for your sin that God paid for you with His Son.

John 3:16 says, "For God so loved the world that He gave His one and only Son, that whoever believes in Him will not perish but have eternal life." And the Apostle Paul declared in Romans 5:8, "But God demonstrates His own love towards us, in that while we were yet sinners, Christ died for us."

"C" – *Commit your life to Jesus Christ*. There is an old bumper sticker that was very popular many years ago that said, "God is my Co-Pilot". That is a great bumper sticker, but it is not what needs to happen in your life to be saved. You must make God the Pilot of your life.

The best you can understand, you must give God your life and make Him the Boss of your life. It is not a checklist of "dos and don'ts". It is a heart issue of having faith that your life is in better hands with God leading rather than with you leading.

Since I gave my life to Christ in 1991, He has been the Boss of my life. Now, I surrender to Him every day and really every minute of every day. Giving your life to Christ means you have faith that He died for your sin, and you are committing your life to Him.

The Bible says in Romans 10:9-10, "that if you confess with your mouth Jesus as Lord and believe in your heart God raised Him from the dead, you will be saved; for with the heart a person believes, resulting in righteousness and with the mouth he confesses resulting in salvation."

Being saved means we are saved from our sin and the separation from God caused by that sin. We are saved from the punishment of sin in a place called hell. We are saved to God to become His child. Let me encourage you to think through this.

If you want to receive Christ as your Lord and Savior, then you can pray a simple prayer like,

"Lord, forgive me of my sins and I know that I am a sinner. I believe that Jesus died on a cross for my sins and I ask Jesus to come into my heart and be the Boss of my life. Jesus, save me."

Now, if you prayed that, please get in touch with someone at a local church or look me up on Facebook or at my church (Cypress Baptist Church, Benton, LA).

Being a Champion does not mean you always win. Being a true champion in Christ does mean we will have the final victory. My prayer for you is you put your head down and get after "it", whatever "it" is. Go for the win and shoot for the stars! Do not settle for being average or the participation trophy. Be a champion!!!

"Being a true champion is about you giving your life to Jesus Christ."

About the Author

Pastor John Fream is a native of Midwest City, Oklahoma. He received his Bachelor of Science from Southern Nazarene University and his Master of Divinity from Southern Baptist Theological Seminary. Pastor John was saved in 1991 and soon after accepted the call into ministry. He served in Student Ministry for 8 years before becoming Lead Pastor at Calvary Baptist in Broken Arrow, OK in 2002.

In 2008, Pastor John was called to Cypress Baptist Church, a church surrounded by cow pastures in the small town of Benton, LA. Under John's leadership and by the goodness of God, Cypress has seen remarkable growth with baptisms almost weekly.

John and his wife Darla of 36 years, have two children. Their daughter, Megan and her husband Kevin have two children, Rhett and Mary Lou. John and Darla love being grandparents and dote on them any chance they get. Their son Brad and his wife Sarah were married last year and are both starting their careers. Pastor John is an avid reader, hunter, and sports fan, with a special place in his heart for Oklahoma football.

Go Sooners!

www.ingramcontent.com/pod-product-compliance
Lightning Source LLC
Chambersburg PA
CBHW050043080526
44586CB00014B/1427